THE CHEAT CODE TO
REENTRY HIRING

A Guide for Employers, HR Leaders
& Workforce Developers

Jonas Royster & Armand King

PARADISE
PUBLISHING COMPANY

P A R A D I S E
PUBLISHING COMPANY

For permissions contact:
info@hoodproverbz.com
Jonas Royster
30450 Haun Road #1041
Menifee, CA 92584
jonasroyster@hoodproverbz.com
www.hoodproverbz.com

Printed Worldwide
First Printing 2025
First Edition 2025
ISBN: 979-8-9887279-6-5

Co-Published by Hood Proverbz and Walk With Me Impact Media &
Education in association with Paradise Publishing Company

Table of Contents

Welcome Letter from Jonas Royster..4

Why Hire Reentry Talent? 7

The Tangible Street Résumé:
Unpacking Transferable Skills..10

The Intangible Street Résumé:
Unpacking Transferable Values 14

The 'Cheat Code' Mindset:
What Makes These Individuals Valuable Employees 20

How to Recruit Justice-Impacted &
Street-Experienced Talent...23

What to Look for in Interviews...28

Creating a Supportive & Empowering Workplace Culture................32

Accountability Without Alienation..37

Risk Management & HR Guidance...41

What's In It for Employers?...45

Don't Sleep on Entrepreneurship:
A Critical Piece of the Reentry Puzzle...48

The Employer & Educator Toolkit...56

Final Message: Be the Door That Opens......................................61

Let's Connect 63

Welcome Letter from Jonas Royster

Co-Author of The Cheat Code to Reentry Hiring

Dear Reader,

Thank you for choosing to open this guide.

Whether you are a workforce developer, HR leader, hiring manager, or social impact advocate, your presence here signals something more than compliance; it signals that you care. It suggests that you are not only open to new strategies but also open to people. And in the reentry space, that openness is the difference between opportunity and another closed door.

This guide is not just informational; it is transformational. It is an invitation to see justice-impacted individuals through a sharper, more human lens. One that recognizes potential not as a possibility, but as a present reality that systems have historically overlooked.

Why I Do This Work

I do not approach this work from theory; I come to it from lived experience.

Years ago, I made the decision to rebuild my life, not just to step away from the bad decision-making that constantly led to incarceration, but to step fully into my purpose. I knew I had more to offer. But as I began the process of reintegration, I quickly learned that having value is not enough if the world refuses to see it.

Like many others, I was told directly and indirectly that the skills that I sharpened while operating outside of the law for twenty-plus years were worth nothing in corporate America. That my past erased my potential. But when I paused long enough to look inward, I realized what many employers fail to see:

What the world labeled as survival was, in fact, strategy.
What they called dysfunction was discipline under pressure.
And what they assumed was a deficit was actually undeveloped leadership.

That internal realization became my breakthrough. And over time, that breakthrough became a framework—*The Cheat Code*. A tool to help individuals translate their lived experiences into professional value, and to help employers recognize what's too often hidden behind the label of "justice-impacted."

Why This Guide Matters

This guide is designed to help you hire differently and lead better.

Inside, you'll discover how to identify transferable skills, assess emotional intelligence, and create a values-based hiring model that centers both character and competence. You'll also find a deeper understanding of how healing, accountability, and personal development can shape a candidate's readiness more than a résumé ever could.

This isn't about lowering standards.
It's about *elevating your lens*.
It's about building stronger teams by expanding how we define readiness, reliability, and resilience. Because justice-impacted individuals are not liabilities waiting to be managed, they are assets waiting to be recognized.

Let's Shift the Narrative Together

Fair-chance hiring is not charity; it is innovation. It is workforce development with *depth*. It is community building with *intention*.

This guide was created for leaders who don't just want to do good—they want to do better. Leaders who believe that equity is not an extra, but an essential.

So let's lead that way together.
Let's change how we hire.
Let's change how we see.
Let's change the reentry game for good.

With clarity and commitment,

— Jonas Royster
Hood Proverbz | The Cheat Code Experience

Why Hire Reentry Talent?

The Business Case You Can't Afford to Ignore

Every year, more than **600,000 individuals return home from incarceration in the United States.** Nearly **1 in 3 American adults** has a criminal record of some kind. Despite this, a staggering number remain locked out of opportunity, not by prison bars—but by employment barriers, outdated policies, and misconceptions.

According to the Prison Policy Initiative, the unemployment rate for formerly incarcerated people is **over 27%,** which is higher than the national rate during the Great Depression. For Black men with records, the numbers are even worse.

But here's what most employers miss:
These numbers don't reflect a lack of work ethic, motivation, or ability. They reflect a lack of access.

That's where forward-thinking employers, HR professionals, and workforce leaders come in. The ones ready to tap into one of the most overlooked—and most loyal—talent pools in the nation.

Breaking Down Myths vs. Realities

Let's address the elephants in the room. Many employers hesitate to hire justice-impacted individuals because of fear, stigma, or misunderstanding. Here's what's actually true:

Myth	Reality
"They'll reoffend or create problems at work."	Studies show that second-chance employees have **equal or better retention rates** and are **no more likely to be terminated** than other workers.
"They lack job skills or experience."	Many have **highly transferable skills** from informal or street economies: logistics, sales, leadership, risk management, and more.
"It's a liability to hire someone with a record."	With the right policies, it's no more risky than any other hire. Plus, there are legal protections and tax incentives.
"It's a charity move, not a business one."	Second-chance hiring is **not charity** — it's **smart business** and **inclusive leadership**.

The Moral Obligation — and the Economic Opportunity

We often hear that people deserve a "second chance," but here's the reality:
Most of them never got a fair first one.

Justice-impacted individuals often come from under-resourced communities shaped by generational poverty, over-policing, and systemic neglect. When they return home, they don't just face barriers—they face brick walls.

Giving someone a real opportunity to earn, contribute, and grow is about more than workforce development — it's about **community restoration.** It's about public safety. And it's about equity.

But let's be clear: this isn't just a feel-good cause — **it's an economic win.**

Here's why:

- **Higher retention:** Many reentry hires are deeply loyal. When treated fairly, they tend to stay longer and work harder.

- **Tax incentives:** The Work Opportunity Tax Credit (WOTC) can provide up to $2,400 per eligible hire.

- **Broader talent pool:** In a time of labor shortages, tapping into this workforce expands your options.

- **Community brand boost:** Companies that lead with inclusion earn consumer trust, employee morale, and media respect.

In Summary: Why You?

Because you don't just fill positions — you **build futures.**

Because when you give someone a real opportunity after incarceration, you're not just reducing recidivism — you're investing in a workforce that knows the value of a second chance.

And because the employers who step up now will be the ones remembered for doing the right thing — at the right time.

"Hiring reentry talent isn't risky. Ignoring it is."

The Tangible Street Résumé: Unpacking Transferable Skills

Most hiring managers are trained to look for polished résumés, corporate experience, and formal education. But when it comes to formerly incarcerated or street-experienced individuals, many of the most valuable skills are hidden in plain sight—unwritten, unrecognized, but deeply developed through lived experience.

What some dismiss as "criminal history" often masks **raw talent, survival intelligence, and untapped leadership.** These individuals may not have climbed corporate ladders, but they've navigated high-stakes environments, led complex operations, and learned to adapt quickly in the face of adversity.

Let's break down the real value behind the street résumé.

Leadership

Whether it's organizing a crew, running an informal business, or managing life inside a system of control, many reentry individuals have already functioned as **natural leaders** — just not in traditional roles.

They've:

- Delegated tasks under pressure

- Motivated peers with limited resources

- Navigated power dynamics and interpersonal politics

- Kept people focused and operational under chaos

What it means for you as an employer:
These are the people who can lead teams, take initiative, and hold others accountable. They know how to step up when it matters.

Conflict Resolution

When survival depends on how you manage confrontation, conflict resolution becomes a life skill — not a training module.

Many justice-impacted individuals:

- Learn how to de-escalate high-stress situations

- Manage interpersonal tensions across backgrounds and personalities

- Mediate disputes and build alliances

- Operate with emotional intelligence in hostile environments

What it means for you:
These employees are equipped to handle workplace tension, mediate between coworkers, and stay cool under pressure. With proper structure, they often become peacemakers in your workplace culture.

Sales and Persuasion

Let's keep it real: anyone who has ever had to "move product" in the streets has already mastered the core elements of sales.

They understand:

- **Target demographics**

- Building trust and rapport

- Marketing under constraints

- Reading body language and adjusting pitches on the fly

- Closing deals with confidence and strategy

What it means for you:
With coaching and legal direction, these same skills transition seamlessly into roles in customer service, sales, outreach, and fundraising. You're not starting from scratch — you're just redirecting hustle.

Operational Strategy

What looks like "running game" on the outside often involves serious strategic thinking behind the scenes.

Many reentry individuals have:

- Planned and executed logistics operations

- Tracked supply chains and cash flow

- Organized and protected assets

- Created efficient systems with minimal tools

What it means for you:
You're looking at potential operations managers, warehouse supervisors, logistics planners, and team leads. They just need a legal blueprint and a supportive structure.

Work Ethic and Grit

Surviving the streets — and the system — requires a level of grit most people can't imagine.

Justice-impacted individuals often:

- Wake up with a survival mindset every day

- Push through hardship without quitting

- Handle rejection and failure without giving up

- Adapt quickly and work long hours without complaint

What it means for you:
Once given an opportunity, these individuals often outperform traditional hires in commitment, endurance, and motivation. They're hungry — not just for a job, but for transformation.

Critical Thinking

When every decision could affect your safety or freedom, you learn to think deeper—faster. Critical thinking is sharpened by survival, not softened by it.

Many justice-impacted individuals:

- Analyze risks and outcomes before making a move

- Break down complex situations and assess the best path

- Think beyond the moment and consider long-term consequences

- Reflect on past outcomes to inform better choices in the future

What it means for you:
These employees bring real-time problem-solving, strategic awareness, and instinctive decision-making. With coaching and clarity, they become reliable thinkers who don't just react—they respond with purpose.

The Intangible Street Résumé: Unpacking Transferable Values

These aren't just soft skills—they're lived values. Forged in high-pressure environments and earned through experience, these values are often misunderstood or overlooked. But when given structure and support, they become a foundation for excellence in any professional setting.

Below are six of the most powerful values individuals returning from incarceration often carry—and what they mean for your workplace:

Honesty

When freedom has been lost and reclaimed, truth becomes a code. Honesty isn't just about telling the truth—it's about being real, being accountable, and owning your decisions.

Many justice-impacted individuals:

- Speak with transparency and directness

- Value truth over ego, even when it's uncomfortable

- Own their past without shame or sugarcoating

- Choose accountability over avoidance

What it means for you:
These employees don't play games. They're straight shooters who bring clarity to your team. In roles that require trust, discretion, or feedback—honesty isn't a bonus, it's a baseline.

Loyalty

When trust is scarce, loyalty becomes everything. The commitment to stand by those who stand by you runs deep—and when that loyalty is earned, it's unshakable.

Many justice-impacted individuals:

- Protect and advocate for those they trust

- Prioritize team success over personal shine

- Show up consistently, even through hard times

- Form strong bonds with mentors, supervisors, and peers

What it means for you:
When you invest in them, they invest back. Loyalty fuels retention, team cohesion, and a sense of ownership that can't be taught—it's lived.

Integrity

Doing the right thing—even when no one's watching—hits different when you've already faced the consequences of doing wrong. Integrity is about living with intention and walking your talk.

Many justice-impacted individuals:

- Make decisions based on principles, not pressure

- Hold themselves accountable for actions and impact

- Reject shortcuts that compromise their character

- Stay aligned with their personal growth and values

What it means for you:
These employees carry moral weight. You can count on them to represent your brand, follow through on commitments, and own their role with pride.

Discipline

When your freedom has depended on routine, consistency, and staying out of trouble, discipline becomes more than a trait—it's a lifeline.

Many justice-impacted individuals:

- Follow structure and routine with precision

- Set personal goals and stick to them

- Choose delayed gratification over quick wins

- Push through discomfort to get results

What it means for you:
They show up early. They finish what they start. And they don't fold under pressure. With the right environment, discipline turns into dependable execution.

Commitment

They've committed to change. Committed to growth. Committed to a different future. This isn't just about words—it's backed by sacrifice and follow-through.

Many justice-impacted individuals:

- Stay loyal to second chances and those who provide them

- Work hard to rebuild trust—professionally and personally

- Stick with tough jobs, knowing what's at stake

- Take pride in keeping their word

What it means for you:
These are employees who don't quit when it gets hard. They bring grit, focus, and a long-term mindset that adds real stability to your team.

Adaptability

When every environment demands a new survival strategy, flexibility becomes second nature. Justice-impacted individuals learn how to read the room—and adjust fast.

Many justice-impacted individuals:

- Pivot quickly when plans change

- Pick up new systems, language, and routines with ease

- Blend into diverse teams and environments

- Thrive in roles that require resilience and quick learning

What it means for you:
These individuals don't panic under pressure. They adapt, evolve, and keep moving forward—making them invaluable in fast-paced or ever-changing work settings.

Cindy S. – From Street Hustle to Executive Leadership

Cindy entered one of my earliest workforce development programs—CHAMP, a culinary-based initiative that blended job training, entrepreneurship, and life skills. At the time, Cindy was reentering society after over a decade of incarceration tied to street-level commerce and survival. She'd been in and out of institutions since her teens, convinced she had no options outside of what she'd always known.

But something shifted. Cindy committed to learning, healing, and finding a company that would see beyond her record and recognize her value. It wasn't easy. Rejections piled up. But then one company—a progressive insurance firm—gave her a chance.

She started in an entry-level role and, within a short time, helped them increase profits tenfold. Today, Cindy is one of their top executive leaders, helping shape company culture and growth strategies. She rarely looks back, but her journey is a living testament to what's possible when employers see people, not just paper.

Maclovio M. – From System-Involved Youth to Fitness Mentor and Motivational Speaker

Maclovio received his high school diploma behind the walls of juvenile detention. By 19, he was homeless, addicted, and entangled in the generational cycles of gangs and substance use that had shaped his family for years. Society expected him to fail.

When he joined my reentry workforce development program, it wasn't a smooth start. But Maclovio didn't quit. He volunteered. He stayed consistent. And he showed up—not just for the program, but for himself.

Today, Maclovio is a certified fitness instructor, working in gyms across San Diego County. He's also a motivational speaker and youth mentor, sharing his story with students in schools across the country. His transformation is no fluke—it's the product of resilience, opportunity, and the kind of belief that can only grow when someone is given a real shot.

Bottom Line:
 If you're only looking at what's on paper, you're going to miss some of the **most naturally gifted, high-potential workers available today.**

These aren't just redemptive stories — they're high-return investments. When you learn how to read the street résumé, you unlock a pipeline of **resilient, loyal, and highly coachable team members** who are just waiting to be seen.

"They don't need saving — they need hiring."

The 'Cheat Code' Mindset: What Makes These Individuals Valuable Employees

Hiring someone with a justice-impacted or street background isn't just about doing a good deed—it's about unlocking a mindset shaped by struggle, resilience, and determination. When given a real opportunity, many of these individuals bring a level of commitment, loyalty, and hunger that's hard to find elsewhere.

This isn't theory. It's what employers who have taken the chance are already seeing: people with something to prove, and everything to gain.

Loyalty and Long-Term Retention

In a time when turnover costs businesses billions, loyalty is a rare and valuable trait. Justice-impacted individuals who are given meaningful employment often show deep commitment to the companies that took a chance on them.

They're less likely to job-hop. They often view the position not just as a paycheck, but as a fresh start. When a workplace treats them with fairness and respect, many respond with long-term dedication, dependability, and a willingness to grow.

Gratefulness for Second Chances

Most people with records know what it feels like to be overlooked, judged, or dismissed. So when they are seen as more than their past—and are given a legitimate chance to succeed—they don't take it lightly.

This gratitude shows up in how they show up. Many work harder, arrive earlier, and stay later. They care about proving themselves, not just to their employer, but to their family, community, and themselves.

Gratitude becomes fuel. It becomes pride. And that pride becomes productivity.

Drive to Prove Themselves

There's a fire in someone who's been told they'll never make it.

Many justice-impacted individuals carry a powerful internal drive to change their story. They want to prove wrong every person who doubted them—and more importantly, they want to prove something to the younger generation watching them. That kind of motivation can't be manufactured in a training.

When properly supported, this drive leads to self-improvement, leadership, and a commitment to personal and professional growth.

Street Smarts = Work Smarts (with the Right Support)

The environments many of these individuals come from have sharpened their instincts, adaptability, and problem-solving skills. They've learned to read people, adjust quickly, and navigate complex situations with limited resources.

With the right structure, coaching, and clear expectations, those same street smarts easily convert into workplace intelligence.

Where some see a risk, the truth is: many of these individuals already know how to lead, hustle, and think strategically. They just need someone to open the door—and someone willing to see the full value of what they bring through it.

Conclusion

This is the cheat code: hire someone who has already overcome obstacles most people will never face, and you get an employee with something stronger than a polished résumé—you get someone with resilience, gratitude, and grit.

That's not just a good hire. That's a competitive edge.

How to Recruit Justice-Impacted & Street-Experienced Talent

Building a diverse, resilient, and loyal workforce starts with where—and how—you recruit. Justice-impacted and street-experienced individuals often don't come through traditional channels like LinkedIn or college career fairs. They exist in parallel systems, often overlooked by standard recruitment practices.

To access this untapped pool of talent, you'll need to think differently. Recruitment for this population must be intentional, relational, and rooted in trust. Here's how to get started.

Partner with Reentry Programs and Community-Based Organizations

One of the most direct and effective recruitment strategies is to build relationships with organizations that already serve this population. These are the trusted spaces where justice-impacted individuals go for reentry support, employment assistance, housing, and mentorship.

Look for:

- Reentry nonprofit organizations

- Workforce development agencies with reentry components

- Transitional housing and sober living programs

- Faith-based organizations that support returning citizens

- Violence prevention and restorative justice initiatives

- Local chapters of national programs (e.g., Center for Employment Opportunities, Defy Ventures)

Reach out to program directors and staff, introduce your company, and explain your desire to hire from the reentry community. These partnerships often produce highly motivated referrals and help establish long-term pipelines of talent.

Leverage Parole, Probation, and Job Developer Networks

Parole and probation departments are often in contact with hundreds of justice-involved individuals actively looking for employment. Many of them also employ job developers, reentry specialists, or community supervision officers whose role is to connect clients with opportunities.

Contact:

- County parole/probation offices

- Department of Corrections reentry divisions

- Day reporting centers

- Community corrections case managers

Be clear about what your company offers, what roles are available, and what level of background check (if any) will be required. Offering a consistent point of contact or attending their employment events can go a long way in building trust and visibility.

Write Inclusive and Trauma-Informed Job Postings

A job description is often the first (and sometimes only) signal to justice-impacted individuals that a company is open to them. The wrong language can immediately deter a qualified person from applying—even when they'd be a great fit.

Tips for inclusive job descriptions:

- Remove blanket exclusions like "must have a clean background"

- Include a line like: "We welcome applications from individuals with justice system involvement"

- Focus on required skills and character traits, not arbitrary credentials

- Avoid corporate jargon that may alienate applicants unfamiliar with traditional workplace culture

- Be clear about the support and growth opportunities offered

It's also important to consider your online presence. If your careers page or website uses inclusive language and reflects real diversity, justice-impacted individuals are more likely to feel that they belong.

Where to Find Credible Referrals

One of the most effective and sustainable ways to recruit this population is through **lived experience mentors** and community connectors—individuals who have walked that path and now serve as bridges between the streets and the workforce.

These credible messengers often work within:

- Community-based organizations

- Youth violence prevention teams

- Housing or sober living programs

- Street outreach and gang intervention groups

- Grassroots mentoring and life coaching programs

Many of these mentors are already trusted by those seeking employment and can personally vouch for individuals who are ready to work, grow, and contribute.

Consider:

- Hosting small, invite-only hiring info sessions led by these mentors

- Offering early access to job openings for their referrals

- Including them in the onboarding process as informal support

Their involvement not only strengthens recruitment—it also reinforces retention by creating a sense of accountability and belonging for the new hire.

Recruiting justice-impacted and street-experienced individuals isn't about charity—it's about connection, strategy, and intentionality. The talent is out there. But it won't walk through the door unless the door is clearly open.

When you build real partnerships, use inclusive language, and tap into trusted networks, you don't just fill jobs—you change lives and strengthen your workforce in ways that go far beyond a résumé.

This isn't just recruitment. It's transformation. And it starts with the way you choose to look for talent.

What to Look for in Interviews

Hiring someone from a justice-impacted or street-involved background often means **looking past what's missing on paper** and instead focusing on the potential in front of you. A traditional résumé might not tell the full story — but a conversation can.

The interview is your chance to uncover the lived experience, emotional intelligence, and raw skill that rarely fits neatly into a job application. But to do that effectively, you'll need to approach the process with the right lens and ask the right questions.

Beyond the Résumé: Asking Questions That Reveal Value

Standard interview questions like "Tell me about your last job" or "Where do you see yourself in five years?" often fall flat for justice-impacted applicants — not because they lack vision or work ethic, but because their paths haven't followed conventional lines.

Instead, try questions that tap into their strengths, life experiences, and problem-solving abilities. Examples include:

- "Tell me about a time when you had to solve a tough problem with limited resources."

- "How have you handled conflict or tension in past situations?"

- "What do you think makes you a good teammate or leader?"

- "Can you describe a time when you had to motivate others or keep them focused?"

- "What does a second chance mean to you, and how would you make the most of it here?"

These kinds of questions help you see behind the surface and hear how a candidate thinks, adapts, and leads — regardless of where those lessons were learned.

Recognizing Emotional Intelligence, Resilience, and Resourcefulness

Justice-impacted individuals have often navigated extreme adversity. The interview is your opportunity to assess not just technical qualifications, but **soft skills** that can be even more valuable in the workplace.

Here's what to listen and look for:

- **Emotional Intelligence:** Do they show awareness of how their past actions affected others? Do they express accountability, humility, or empathy? Can they read a room or sense group dynamics?

- **Resilience:** Have they overcome setbacks, rejection, or trauma? Do they express hope, determination, or forward-looking mindsets?

- **Resourcefulness:** Have they figured things out without formal training? Do they describe learning through trial and error, self-teaching, or creative problem-solving?

You're not just hiring for **where someone's been — you're hiring for where they're ready to go.**

How to Avoid Unconscious Bias During Hiring

Even the most well-meaning employers can unknowingly let bias creep into the interview process. For justice-impacted individuals, this can mean being judged more harshly for things that have nothing to do with their ability to perform the job.

Tips to reduce unconscious bias:

- **Don't lead with "Tell me about your record."** If background checks are required, they'll come later. Focus the interview on skills, values, and fit.

- **Avoid assumptions about gaps.** Many individuals have gaps in employment due to incarceration or survival circumstances. Ask about what they learned during that time instead of treating it as a red flag.

- **Standardize the process.** Use the same set of core questions for all applicants to ensure fairness and consistency.

- **Train your hiring team.** Make sure everyone involved understands the barriers justice-impacted applicants face and the value they bring.

- **Focus on potential over polish.** A lack of professional lingo or formal credentials doesn't equal a lack of capability. Listen for grit, not grammar.

If you're only looking for the candidate who interviews like a polished professional, you'll miss the one who could become your most loyal, driven, and resilient employee.

The interview isn't about checking boxes — it's about opening doors. When you shift your questions and mindset, you'll be surprised by what you find on the other side.

You're not just interviewing for a position — you're interviewing for transformation. And it starts by seeing the value others overlook.

Creating a Supportive & Empowering Workplace Culture

Hiring a justice-impacted or street-experienced individual is only the first step. **Retention, development, and long-term transformation** happen when the work environment is intentionally supportive, empowering, and trauma-informed.

These individuals often bring not only resilience but also invisible wounds—years of instability, mistrust, or survival-mode thinking. If your workplace culture doesn't reflect understanding and safety, you risk reinforcing past harm rather than creating new opportunities.

Here's how to build a culture where formerly incarcerated or street-involved employees don't just survive—but thrive.

Trauma-Informed Onboarding Practices

The onboarding experience sets the tone. For justice-impacted individuals, traditional orientation processes can feel rigid, impersonal, or even intimidating. Trauma-informed onboarding makes space for vulnerability, learning curves, and the unique lived experiences your new hires bring.

Key elements include:

- **Warm welcomes over paperwork first:** Build connection before compliance. Introduce the person to team members, give a tour, and show them they belong.

- **Be clear, not cold:** Avoid assuming prior knowledge. Break down expectations in simple, respectful terms without corporate jargon.

- **Assign a point person:** Someone who checks in during the first 30–60 days can help prevent misunderstandings, confusion, or unnecessary anxiety.

- **Explain structure as support:** Many justice-impacted people have come from rigid systems (prison, court, parole). Show how your structure is meant to support success, not control or punish.

When onboarding is relational and empowering, it lowers anxiety, builds trust, and increases retention from day one.

Establishing Psychological Safety

Psychological safety is the foundation of a high-performing, inclusive workplace. It means your team members feel safe to speak up, ask questions, admit mistakes, or be vulnerable— without fear of embarrassment, punishment, or judgment.

For justice-impacted individuals, who may be used to operating in hyper-vigilant, high-stakes environments, creating psychological safety takes intentional effort.

Tips to build it:

- **Model transparency and humility:** Leaders who admit their own mistakes or ask for feedback normalize that behavior for others.

- **Respond, don't react:** When an employee brings up a concern or makes a misstep, prioritize listening and support over punishment.

- **Watch for trauma responses:** Defensive behavior, withdrawal, or mistrust may be signs of past harm. Respond with curiosity, not critique.

- **Foster peer support:** When team members look out for each other, safety grows exponentially.

Psychological safety increases engagement, creativity, and retention—especially for those who've never worked in environments where they were truly valued.

Creating Structured Growth Paths

Justice-impacted individuals are often hired into entry-level roles but never shown a clear way to advance. Without growth, even the most motivated employees can plateau or disengage.

Show your team what's possible by:

- **Mapping out career paths:** Share what advancement looks like within your company and what steps lead there.

- **Offering incremental goals:** Breaking progress into clear milestones gives people something to work toward and builds confidence.

- **Recognizing and rewarding growth:** Catch people doing things right. Celebrate progress, not just perfection.

- **Providing upskilling opportunities:** Offer trainings, certifications, or job-shadowing options so employees can expand their value.

When people see a future with your company, they invest more in the present.

Mentorship, Buddy Systems, and Lived Experience Support

One of the most powerful ways to create a supportive culture is by **connecting justice-impacted employees with people who understand their journey.**

This could look like:

- **Peer mentorship:** Pairing new hires with longer-term employees—especially those with similar lived experience—creates safety, accountability, and trust.

- **Buddy systems:** Assigning a "go-to" team member for day-to-day questions builds confidence and reduces isolation.

- **Lived experience staff support:** Consider hiring or training credible messengers (mentors who have navigated reentry successfully) to serve as on-site or on-call support for justice-impacted employees.

- **Monthly check-ins:** Even a short, structured time to reflect and get feedback can go a long way in supporting emotional and professional stability.

People don't grow in isolation—they grow in relationship. Mentorship and support systems create the community necessary for long-term success.

Creating a supportive workplace culture isn't about being soft—it's about being **strategic, intentional, and human.** The strongest teams are built not just on skill, but on connection, trust, and belonging.

When your workplace becomes a place of healing and growth, you don't just retain employees—you unlock potential that can transform your entire organization.

Support is the new leadership. And culture is the new competitive advantage.

Accountability Without Alienation

Hiring someone from a justice-impacted or street-influenced background does not mean lowering your standards—it means raising your **capacity to lead with compassion, clarity, and purpose.**

For many individuals in this population, rules have often been used as weapons, not tools. They've lived under systems that punished without explanation and rejected without opportunity. So when they enter a new job, the way accountability is handled can either reinforce old trauma—or become part of their transformation.

The goal isn't to avoid tough conversations—it's to have them **without shame, blame, or alienation.** Here's how to do that effectively.

Clear Expectations + Second Chances

One of the most common breakdowns in employment with justice-impacted workers isn't a lack of willingness—**it's a lack of clarity.**

Make sure expectations are:

- **Written, visible, and consistent** from day one

- Explained with both **the "what" and the "why"**

- Reinforced regularly through check-ins and feedback

- Reviewed with understanding of learning curves and emotional adjustment

Clear expectations prevent misunderstanding. And when mistakes happen—as they will with any employee—justice-impacted workers should be offered **a second chance with support,** not immediate discipline.

Second chances are not about ignoring issues; they're about providing guidance and showing that one mistake doesn't equal a dead end.

Coaching vs. Punishing

Traditional discipline models often trigger shame, shutdown, or rebellion in individuals who have experienced punitive systems. Instead of resorting to warnings or write-ups as your first move, try **coaching as your leadership style.**

Coaching means:

- Addressing the behavior, not attacking the person

- Asking open-ended questions before making assumptions

- Offering strategies to improve, rather than focusing on what went wrong

- Sharing your investment in their success, not just your authority

For example, instead of saying:
"You were late again. You need to fix this or you're out."

Try:
"I noticed you were late again today. Can we talk about what's going on? I want to help you figure out how to succeed here, and punctuality is part of that. What support do you need?"

This doesn't mean excusing ongoing issues—but it creates a space where people can **own their behavior without fear** of being discarded.

How to Have Tough Conversations with Compassion

Tough conversations are part of leadership. But when dealing with justice-impacted employees, how you approach them can make or break trust.

Tips for leading with compassion:

- **Stay calm and present.** Your tone matters as much as your words.

- **Lead with curiosity, not control.** Ask what's behind the behavior instead of jumping to conclusions.

- **Normalize mistakes as growth moments.** Everyone has setbacks—what matters is how we respond to them.

- **Affirm their value.** Remind the person that they matter to the team, even if correction is needed.

You can say hard things with a soft heart. And when people feel respected—even in correction—they're far more likely to change, grow, and stay.

Accountability doesn't have to mean alienation. It can mean growth, development, and transformation—**if it's rooted in relationship and respect.**

When employers shift from a punishment model to a coaching mindset, they don't just retain more employees—they help reshape how those employees see themselves.

The cheat code isn't just about hiring differently—it's about leading differently. And that's where real change begins.

Risk Management & HR Guidance

Fair-chance hiring doesn't mean hiring blindly. It means hiring **intelligently and inclusively,** with systems in place that balance accountability, opportunity, and compliance.

Employers often hesitate to bring on justice-impacted or street-experienced individuals out of fear—fear of liability, public perception, or disruption. But with proper planning and HR alignment, these risks are manageable, and the rewards are significant.

This section walks you through key legal frameworks, policy shifts, and HR practices to help your organization implement fair-chance hiring in a way that is both ethical and strategic.

Legal Protections & Compliance (EEOC, Ban the Box, WOTC)

Employers are often unaware of the legal protections that **encourage** the hiring of people with records—or the risks of violating them through exclusionary practices.
Key legal concepts to know:

- EEOC Guidance: The U.S. Equal Employment Opportunity Commission prohibits blanket bans on hiring individuals with criminal records. Employers must evaluate applicants individually, considering:
  - The nature and gravity of the offense
  - The time passed since the conviction
  - The nature of the job

  Denial must be based on business necessity, not generalizations.

- **Ban the Box Laws:** These laws prohibit employers from asking about criminal history on job applications or conducting background checks until after a conditional job offer. Many states, counties, and cities have adopted these policies. Know your local laws—and comply.

- **Work Opportunity Tax Credit (WOTC):** The WOTC is a federal tax credit available to employers who hire individuals from targeted groups, including people with felony records. The credit can be worth up to **$2,400 per qualifying hire.** Employers can apply by submitting IRS Form 8850 and ETA Form 9061.

Understanding these frameworks helps you avoid liability, tap into incentives, and comply with modern fair-chance hiring standards.

Company Policy Adjustments That Remove Barriers

Your internal policies can either create opportunity—or quietly block it.

If you want to support justice-impacted and street-experienced workers, take a fresh look at your hiring and employment policies through a fair-chance lens.

Common adjustments include:

- **Revising background check language:** Instead of "must pass a background check," say "background checks will be considered in relation to the role."

- **Removing blanket exclusions:** Avoid automatic disqualifiers like "no felony convictions" unless legally required.

- **Providing appeal processes:** Allow candidates to explain their record, provide references, or share rehabilitation progress.

- **Delaying background checks:** Wait until after the interview or conditional offer to run checks. This ensures the person is evaluated on merit first.

- **Flexible ID requirements:** Some justice-impacted individuals may not immediately have standard forms of ID. Consider alternatives or a grace period where appropriate.

These small shifts can open the door for incredible talent that would otherwise never get a foot in.

Working with HR to Support Fair-Chance Hiring

Your Human Resources team plays a critical role in transforming fair-chance hiring from theory into practice. HR must be involved not only in policy review but in **training, onboarding, and culture-building.**

What HR should prioritize:

- **Fair-chance hiring training for all managers**
  Help your leadership team understand what fair-chance hiring is, why it matters, and how to implement it with equity and consistency.

- **Developing inclusive interview and selection procedures**
  HR can standardize interviews, refine rubrics, and help prevent bias in hiring decisions.

- **Creating clear internal pathways for support**
  HR should establish systems for feedback, coaching, and intervention that prioritize growth, not punishment.

- **Tracking and evaluating outcomes**
  Collect and review data on retention, performance, and engagement of fair-chance hires. Use this to refine policies and build your internal case for continued investment.

Risk doesn't disappear—it gets managed. And in the case of fair-chance hiring, the real risk is missing out on untapped talent due to outdated fears or unchecked bias.

With the right legal knowledge, intentional policy changes, and an aligned HR team, you can build a workplace that's not only compliant—but truly inclusive and forward-thinking.

Fair-chance hiring isn't a risk to mitigate. It's a strategy to lead with.

What's In It for Employers?

Let's be honest—most companies won't change just because it's "the right thing to do." They need to understand the **business value** of hiring justice-impacted and street-experienced individuals. Fortunately, the value is not only real—it's measurable.

Fair-chance hiring isn't about charity or risk—it's about **strategy, loyalty, and leadership.** Companies that lean into this approach see clear returns in productivity, retention, brand reputation, and culture.

Here's what employers gain when they open the door:

Higher Retention Rates

Studies show that justice-impacted employees, when supported properly, have **equal or better retention rates** than their peers. Why? Because for many, this opportunity is more than a job—it's a life-changer.

These individuals often:

- Stay longer because they're grateful for the chance

- Work harder because they want to prove themselves

- Are more likely to remain loyal to employers who treat them fairly

In a job market where turnover is costly and disruptive, retaining skilled and committed team members is a competitive advantage. Fair-chance hires can help you stabilize your workforce.

Strong Team Morale and Loyalty

When a company creates a culture of second chances, it sends a powerful message to *all* employees—that growth is possible, that people matter, and that the company stands for something bigger. The result?

- Increased trust in leadership

- Greater peer support and collaboration

- A workplace where people feel valued and seen

When team members witness a colleague's transformation—or are part of supporting it—it fosters pride, unity, and motivation throughout the company.

Diversity, Equity, and Inclusion Benefits

Justice-impacted individuals are disproportionately from communities of color, low-income backgrounds, and marginalized populations. Hiring from this pool advances your DEI goals in authentic, impactful ways.

But this isn't just about checking a box.

It's about:

- Diversifying not just who you hire, but how you lead

- Learning from lived experiences that bring fresh insight to your teams

- Building equity into your systems, not just your statements

Fair-chance hiring deepens your company's inclusion practices and reflects a genuine commitment to systemic change.

Community Reputation + Tax Incentives

Fair-chance hiring positions your company as a **leader in social responsibility,** workforce development, and economic equity. It enhances your brand and builds goodwill with customers, partners, and the community.

Your company can benefit from:

- Positive media coverage and public recognition

- Increased consumer support for socially responsible businesses

- Strategic partnerships with nonprofit and public sector allies

And let's not forget:
You may also qualify for **Work Opportunity Tax Credits (WOTC)** of up to $2,400 per qualifying hire, putting real dollars back into your bottom line.

Conclusion

The benefits of hiring justice-impacted and street-experienced individuals are not theoretical—they're tangible, practical, and lasting.

When you embrace fair-chance hiring, you're not lowering your standards—you're raising your company's potential.

It's not just about changing lives.
It's about changing the way business gets done—for the better.

Don't Sleep on Entrepreneurship: A Critical Piece of the Reentry Puzzle

"Don't just teach a man to fish — show him how to start a fishing business."

Who this is for:

- Reentry educators

- Workforce developers

- Employment program coordinators

- Transitional housing/job readiness staff

If you're in the business of helping justice-impacted individuals reintegrate into society, you're also in the business of **restoring agency, identity, and income.** And for many, that path won't be through a traditional 9-to-5. It will be through entrepreneurship.

This section isn't about replacing job readiness with business ownership. It's about recognizing that for many formerly incarcerated or street-experienced individuals, entrepreneurship may be their most **realistic, natural, and liberating path forward.**

Why Entrepreneurship Matters for This Population

Many justice-impacted individuals have never had a "real job"— but that doesn't mean they've never worked. On the contrary, many have already:

- Managed logistics

- Handled customer relations

- Negotiated supply and demand

- Scaled small enterprises under the radar

What they were missing wasn't motivation. It was **legal structure, opportunity, and support.**

And even after release, barriers like background checks, employer stigma, and low-wage ceilings can continue to block access to sustainable employment. Entrepreneurship bypasses these gatekeepers and gives individuals a way to **build something of their own,** with independence and pride.

The Entrepreneurial Skillset Is Already There

The best entrepreneurs aren't always the ones with MBAs. They're often the people who learned how to create value under pressure, move fast, and adapt constantly. For many formerly incarcerated people, this skillset is already deeply embedded— they just need help translating it into a legal and scalable business.

Key traits to nurture:

- **Problem-solving:** Turning obstacles into opportunities

- **Networking:** Building relationships with limited tools and high stakes

- **Marketing:** Knowing your audience and presenting your value clearly

- **Risk management:** Understanding timing, competition, and risk vs. reward

- **Innovation under pressure:** Making something out of nothing, again and again

This is real-world entrepreneurship. And it's already inside many of your clients.

Recommendations for Reentry Programs and Educators

Don't treat entrepreneurship as a bonus topic or afterthought. It should be integrated alongside job training, especially for individuals with leadership potential, creative ideas, or barriers to traditional employment.

Here's how to get started:

- **Offer business fundamentals in accessible, low-barrier formats.**
  Avoid corporate jargon and theory-heavy lectures. Break down the basics: What is a business? How do you price a product? What licenses do you need?

- **Partner with local incubators, co-working spaces, and microloan programs.**
  Create pathways to capital, mentorship, and infrastructure that justice-impacted individuals can tap into.

- **Bring in formerly incarcerated entrepreneurs to teach workshops.**
  Lived experience matters. Seeing someone who looks like them, who has walked that path and built something real, makes entrepreneurship feel possible.

- **Teach how to monetize existing hustle.**
  Help individuals identify what they're already good at—
  cutting hair, designing clothes, cooking, fixing cars—and
  show them how to turn it into a legal business.

- **Integrate entrepreneurship into transitional planning.**
  Don't wait until someone's "job-ready." Start planting seeds
  of ownership early, even during incarceration or early reentry
  phases.

Entrepreneurship isn't a luxury—it's often a necessity. It provides
freedom, purpose, and a legal outlet for ambition that many
justice-impacted individuals already possess.

If you're serious about reducing recidivism, promoting economic
mobility, and unleashing human potential, you can't afford to
sleep on this part of the puzzle.

Jobs change lives. But ownership?
That builds legacies.

Vincent R. – From Reentry to Rising Leadership

Vincent was one of the first participants in our CHAMP
workforce development program back in 2013. At the time, he
had just completed a prison sentence and was still navigating
the complexities of the legal system. Honestly, the odds seemed
stacked against him.

But something powerful happened when Vincent entered the
program. He found structure. He found community. And he
found people who believed in him. With consistent support, he
began to shift his mindset—from survival to strategy. He enrolled
in community college, then transferred and graduated from San
Diego State University.

Today, Vincent works as the Executive Administrative Assistant for a fast-growing consulting firm that trusts him with core operations—logistics, project management, and client coordination. The owner personally told me, "Without Vincent, we wouldn't be functioning the way we are now." He's not just an employee—he's a cornerstone.

Vincent's journey proves what can happen when employers offer a real second chance: they don't just change one life—they gain a leader.

Shanta B. – Street Smarts to CEO

Shanta spent years cycling in and out of jail, hustling to survive. When she finally said "enough," she didn't yet know what her next chapter would look like—only that she didn't want to work for anyone else. She had business instincts, but lacked direction.

Through consistent coaching and mentorship, Shanta discovered her calling. She noticed a gap in the bail bond industry and, drawing from her lived experience, launched her own bail bonds company. Seven years later, her firm is one of the top-performing bail bond businesses in San Diego County—staffed, organized, and thriving.

But she didn't stop there. Shanta is now expanding into real estate and mentorship, using the same hustle and resilience that once helped her survive to now help others succeed. She turned every street-earned skill into a transferable strength—and every "no" into her next "yes."

Randy M. – From Federal Time to Craft Brew Pioneer

At 19, Randy didn't think he had a future. Surrounded by guns, gangs, and drugs, he believed his environment defined him. That mindset led to a federal prison sentence—and a wake-up call.

When Randy returned home, he entered our workforce development program looking for something different. One day, he spotted a job posting at a local craft brewery. I personally connected him with the owner, and they gave him a shot.

Randy didn't just take the opportunity—he ran with it. He moved up to management within two years, and eventually co-created a limited-edition beer for Black History Month. That moment lit a fire. Randy launched his own craft beer brand, which has now been featured at festivals across three countries. He's on his fifth beer release and distributing across California.

Randy's story is proof that when employers make room for returning citizens, they don't just get good workers—they get innovators with unmatched drive.

Ronald R. (Preacher) – From Boostin' to Business

For over three decades, Preacher relied on the street economy to survive—boosting merchandise and flipping it for profit. It was fast money, but it came with a cost: a seven-year state prison sentence and the weight of starting over in his sixties.

When Preacher came home, he didn't need someone to give him value—he needed help *translating it.*

Through one-on-one mentorship and community-based support, he was able to unpack his street résumé and see it for what it truly was: a blueprint of transferable skills and values. He wasn't just surviving—he'd been mastering sales, communication, adaptability, and hustle for decades. The question wasn't if he had talent—it was *how* to apply it.

That's when Preacher leaned in. Despite the digital learning curve, he tapped into entrepreneurial pathways that matched his strengths. He learned how to source legal products from thrift stores, wholesalers, and online platforms. The same grind he used to flip stolen goods now fuels a fully licensed vending business that serves his community with low-cost household essentials.

Today, Preacher isn't just working—he's *building*. He has his own apartment, is earning a master's degree in business management, and continues to grow his business one sale at a time. His story is a testament to what happens when workforce development includes both personal and professional transformation.

When systems see beyond someone's record and into their resourcefulness, they don't just reduce recidivism—they empower legacy-minded entrepreneurs.

Rayshawn R. – From Candy Hustler to High-Earning Entrepreneur

At just 25, Rayshawn R. had already cycled through the system, bounced between hotels, and found himself homeless—sleeping in his car with more questions than answers. His side hustle wasn't bringing in much, and his future felt uncertain.

But what he lacked in resources, he made up for in resilience.

With nothing but a box of candy and an unshakable drive,

Rayshawn tapped into what many overlook: his **street-earned talent for sales.** He set up outside department stores and local malls, moving product with confidence and charisma—skills he had been sharpening long before he ever had a legit business license.

In his first year, he brought in over $60,000 just from selling candy. But he didn't stop there.

Rayshawn came to us ready for elevation. He said, "I know I've got the skill set—but I'm tired of having to sell a hundred $10 items to make the kind of money I want. I'm ready for something bigger."

So, we worked with him to pivot. He took that same **adaptability, communication, and consistency** and launched a **shoe-cleaning business inside malls.** His hustle turned into a brand. That brand turned into a franchise. Today, he **travels the country** running his own business at malls and trade shows, pulling in six figures annually—all while doing what he loves.

Rayshawn is a walking reminder that **workforce development** isn't one-size-fits-all. His **entrepreneurial path** was unlocked by identifying his **transferable skills** and aligning them with a new, legitimate lane.

But more than that, he also leaned into his **transferable values:** belief in himself, faith in his Creator, and the humility to ask for help. His advice to anyone walking that same tightrope? "Don't wait too long to let your gift shine. Your gifts will make room for you—but only if you let them."

Rayshawn's journey proves that when we see justice-impacted talent for who they are—not who they were—we don't just help them earn a living. We help them **build a legacy.**

The Employer & Educator Toolkit

This toolkit is designed to bridge vision and action—for employers looking to hire justice-impacted talent and educators preparing individuals for both employment and entrepreneurship. Whether you're building a hiring strategy or running a reentry program, this section provides hands-on tools to support success.

For Employers: Building a Fair-Chance Hiring Pipeline

Inclusive Job Description Language
Replace exclusionary phrases like:

- "Must pass background check"

- "No felony convictions allowed"

With:

- "We consider all qualified applicants, including individuals with justice involvement."

- "Background checks are conducted on a case-by-case basis and do not automatically disqualify candidates."

Fair-Chance Interview Questions

These help reveal resilience, soft skills, and motivation:

- "Tell me about a time you overcame a major obstacle."

- "How have your past experiences shaped the way you approach work?"

- "What does being part of a team mean to you?"

- "What motivates you to show up and give your best each day?"

- "If given this opportunity, what would success look like for you in 90 days?"

Onboarding Tips

- Assign a peer or lived-experience mentor for the first 30 days

- Break down unwritten workplace rules (e.g., how to ask for help, who to talk to about challenges)

- Provide written and verbal versions of policies and expectations

- Use check-ins weekly for the first month, then monthly afterward

Supportive Policy Checklist

- Delay background checks until after conditional offers

- Offer flexible scheduling when possible

- Create feedback loops (not just evaluations)

- Build partnerships with local reentry orgs for referrals

For Reentry Educators: Preparing for Jobs and Entrepreneurship

Soft Skill Development Areas
Make sure participants are building:

- Communication and active listening

- Emotional regulation

- Time management

- Conflict resolution

- Workplace etiquette

Job Readiness Exercises

- Practice interviews with real employers

- Resume-building workshops (with focus on transferable skills)

- Role-playing difficult workplace scenarios

- Dress-for-success and body language sessions

Sample Questions to Explore Entrepreneurial Readiness
Not everyone is built for business ownership, but many have the foundation. Use these to guide discovery:

- "Have you ever made or sold something on your own?"

- "Do you enjoy coming up with your own ideas and acting on them?"

- "How do you feel about taking risks and learning from mistakes?"

- "Would you prefer the stability of a job or the flexibility of working for yourself?"

- "What's something you're really good at that people already ask you for?"

- "If money and background weren't an issue, what kind of business would you start?"

These questions can reveal mindset, natural talents, and areas for growth.

Shared Tools: Resources & Referrals
Reentry-Friendly Employment Resources

- National HIRE Network: www.hirenetwork.org

- Second Chance Business Coalition: www.secondchancebusinesscoalition.org

- Center for Employment Opportunities (CEO): www.ceoworks.org

- Honest Jobs: www.honestjobs.com

Entrepreneurship Programs for Justice-Impacted Individuals

- Defy Ventures: Entrepreneurship training for people with criminal histories

- Inmates to Entrepreneurs: Free business startup training for formerly incarcerated individuals

- Project ReMADE (Stanford Law School): Business mentorship and training

- Hustle 2.0: Business and leadership curriculum delivered inside and outside institutions

Grant and Microloan Sources

- Kiva Loans (zero-interest microloans, including for justice-involved entrepreneurs)

- Local CDFIs (Community Development Financial Institutions)

- The Fountain Fund: Loans and financial education for formerly incarcerated individuals

- Local SBA offices: Small Business Administration technical assistance and loan access

Mentor & Peer Support Networks

- SCORE: Free business mentoring (nationwide)

- Credible messenger programs (check local community orgs)

- Local reentry task forces and workforce boards

This toolkit is your launchpad. Use it to start conversations, build connections, and implement practices that lead to real transformation—for employees, for program participants, and for your organization.

Hiring changes lives. So does teaching someone how to lead, grow, and own their future.

The tools are here. The change is up to you.

Final Message: Be the Door That Opens

Every day, justice-impacted and street-experienced individuals are ready to work, ready to grow, and ready to contribute. But too often, they're met with closed doors—doors locked by stigma, fear, and outdated systems.

You have the power to change that.

Whether you're an employer making a hiring decision, an HR leader shaping policy, or an educator preparing someone for reentry, you are more than just a professional. You are a potential bridge between someone's past and their future.

This isn't about lowering standards. It's about raising your capacity to see people fully—to recognize that resilience, resourcefulness, and raw potential often come wrapped in nontraditional packages.

Fair-chance hiring isn't just an initiative. It's a mindset. It's a commitment to leading with humanity, to building workplaces that reflect justice as much as they do efficiency.

So ask yourself:

What kind of leader do I want to be? What kind of impact do I want to leave?

Because somewhere right now, there's someone waiting—someone who's done the hard work, changed their mindset, and is just looking for a shot.

Be the one who says yes.
Be the one who sees the value.
Be the door that opens.
— Armand King

Walk With Me Impact | The Cheat Code Experience

Let's Connect

As the old African proverb say's " We can go fast alone, but we can go farther together."

We'd love the opportunity to connect and explore how we can support you and your organization in building upon the impactful work you're doing—or planning to do—with individuals returning from incarceration.

To schedule a meeting or learn more about our services and approach, please don't hesitate to reach out or follow the links below.

Armand L. King

Jonas U. Royster

info@lawrichconsulting.com

jonasroyster@hoodproverbz.com

info@wwmimpact.com

info@hoodproverbzcom

Learn More About the Cheat Code Experience

www.ingramcontent.com/pod-product-compliance
Lightning Source LLC
Chambersburg PA
CBHW071516210326
41597CB00018B/2785